Years

In The Early Life Of A Poet

deadwriter

INTRODUCTION

Inside the heart of every living person there is that yearning to be recognized, to be paid attention to and be loved. A yearning that drives us to seek for that sense of value of our transitory existence and one's sense of belongingness.

Inside our hearts, stories are waiting to be told. Everyone has their own story to tell; for their own journey through life is a story itself. A tiny minuscule part in a much bigger story to tell: the story of man's existence.

This book is about that sense of value that everyone seeks. The emotions, the intangible things that governs us all and the unfulfilled love that keeps us awake at night.

More than just a collection of poetic and philosophical musings, this book is the author's personal journey in understanding life in the early stage of his growth as an artist and profound thinker.

"FOR THE DREAM THAT NEVER CAME"

To Angie
Words are not simply words
We nibble at the tip
Of our tongue's
But thoughts we sleep with
All the while being awake.

[signature]

CONTENTS

Teacher

I Do

I remember waiting for you at the church;

Waiting for you and your friends to show up

A minute after I did.

I remember listening to your voice;

Desperately hoping you will be talking about me.

I remember pretending to be praying

As if it really mattered now.

I remember waiting at the church;

Just so I can look at you as you make your way

To the room where they keep the statues.

I remember the life size statue of Jesus.

Lying inside a glass container

That looked more like a glass coffin to me now.

I remember you being early;

I - hoping you were there waiting for me

To come and find you in that church.

But we never talked.

Nor did I smile looking in your direction.

We never said a word to one another in that church.

We never did.

I remember that.

I still remember you being the love of my life

Twenty years after

And I - married to another.

I wonder if this is infidelity;

Or is this love refusing to die

Even after I said *"I do"*

Inside the very same church

Where I used to wait for you.

Throbbing

The deafening sound of a throbbing pain
Is playing like a broken record now.
Indulging to open up the wounds
Of a past love and bleed to death.
The canvas view of the morning sun
Is painted with blood & hope.

There is nothing much to do but wait
And hope for the best to come along again
As it has when my canvas was still white.

Five hundred years from now
We will see who went too far
Holding on to a cold memory.

Care

Your body
Is like a house.
Be careful who you let in;
Be careful who you let use it.
For in a second
It might be too late to realize
You have been robbed.

Summer Breath

We made love for hours

Her nipples resemble that of two castles.

Our sweat flowed like the current of the Yangtze

While her mouth spat blood onto my candle hands.

Twelve until four

Entwined we float

One we gamble

It is a wonder

How summer could smell

So much like December in a way.

Us

"We came and left;

Suffered the same fate as those who came before us."

Inside

In our own little worlds

We are angels, artisans, sculptors,

Actors and actresses.

We are someone(s) we dream all our lives.

In our own little worlds

We are something we are not;

Yet seemingly possible.

Plates And Paper Bags

Do not put smiles
On an empty plate;
It would only remind you
Of a broken trust.

Never put your insults
In a paper bag;
It would only remind you
How tender she was.

Four Months Of Conversation

Twenty two years old-
Sitting on a chair facing a wall.
Like I always do.

I am amazed how imagination
Could lead to imagining
Green pasture and soft winds.

The four months of conversation we had
Somehow turned me into a twig;
Reaching out for the sky,
Reaching out for the stars.

Everyone has two hearts:
One for longing, One for thinking.
Soaked in oriental
Nectar of compromise.

Memories

Memories hum and sing like children;

As we walked on as if nothing happened.

Teacher

The teacher in me is dead now.

The soul of it has been buried

A thousand times over

Next to my grandmother who died of diabetes.

Too much sweetness in the lines I speak

Drove my lovers away.

"Let me hope & let me live"

The inner voice is screaming;

A voice of a child lost in a sea of people.

Unheard.

But like I said,

The teacher in me is dead now;

No one is around to teach the heart to love again.

Senseless Waiting

You are so far away

I cannot see your face.

In the distance I look upon the possibility

Of abandoning you finally.

The sense in believing you would come back

Is starting to wane off.

Like a cloud escaping from the sight of a child.

Like a broken kite starting to go around in circles.

Senseless flight.

Senseless waiting.

That... I am.

Weeping

"I weep for I am dreaming."

Drunk

I became drunk of the death
Embracing me every night.
It reminds me of your absence;
For it is you I am referring to.

The ever pervading presence of your absence.
The connection between blank spaces
And white lines
And the synapses relaying the message of such.

I became drunk of your literal death;
Your presence in spite of the opposite.

Paddling For Words

There is a sound that reverberates every time I sing.

There is thought of you grabbing the words

Of every song I try to sing;

Making all the songs in the world

Lesser of expression

Devoid of meaning.

There you go again!

Grabbing the words I intend to write

About my childhood treacheries;

Confining me to writing about you instead.

Maybe I should start paddling to shore.

Make my way back to those hands

Stretching

Signaling me for *turnabout*.

It is no use waiting for you here in an empty ocean

Where silence is the only company

Until one loses his mind.

Cellphones And Letters

Nothing could have broken it;
Not even cellphones.

We promised bundle of sweet words,
Only to be broken bit by bit by letters.

It is funny how technology
Can break a heart;
How it could set a flaw
In a relationship.

Technology and letters
A blessing and catastrophe in disguise.

Satin Sky

Entangled by reason and emotions,
I floated around the circus of magic tricks.

Then out of nowhere
You came along

We greeted each other with hellos,
Smiles and sweet glances .

Years passed
Brown residue of time we became;
We have abandoned one another for a while now.

Towards the night sky
Catapulted the thought:
"Somewhere along the vast landscape of existence,
We met."

Home

I can feel you breathing behind my ears

The warmth of your breath

Cradling me to sleep

As you draw each air whispering my name.

My head feels like it is going to burst.

But still... I am listening.

For you comfort me.

Home.

Is what you are

And I am missing you like hell.

Heart

"I came to this place looking for gold;
Only to find my own heart."

Spittle

We should have whispered.

We should have looked at the spittle on our brows
With disregard.

Or maybe

We should have lied about it;

Anyway it was just a card game.

I told her.

She just smiled and said:

" Let us wait for a year or two."

And so I waited.

Where She Stood

I am so tired
She said.

Her eyes gazing at the broken pieces of her past;
Longing to capture the warmth once again.

He left
Without leaving a note;
Same time the neighbors migrated
Somewhere down south.

Everything remained still
In front of their porch
Now lying in ruins.

Including the precious thoughts
Left unsaid.

Sync Beating

I am happy;
I am lonely.

What do you make of that?

I am the happiest loner
In the world.

What do you make of that?

I am utterly alone
In spite of being

With all these people around me.

For it is you I long to be with.

This heart will never know real happiness
Until its beat syncs with yours.

Waterfall

Moving Along

Move on core

Move along my heart.

Move along core

The dusty road leads

To unknown territory.

Romance With Shame

It was my romance with shame

That led me to write this verse;

I craved for something

I can never have.

Something of which I am forbidden to have.

The taste of her skin,

Cocooning the same blood

Running in my vein.

It is forbidden

For it is shameful.

It was my romance with shame

That led me to write this verse.

Words As Reason

I see words as reason;
Reason for me to know hate,
Reason for me to know love.

Words should not be just words
We nibble
At the tip of our tongue as we speak.
Like food, bed, blanket,
Anguish, Hatred, Beauty, Madness.

I find reason in words;
Reason for my being.

Philosophy

Your breasts hang like clouds

In a starry night sky;

I am a child feeding on your disease.

Frame

I was reading Hayakawa's
Use and Misuse of Language
When I remember
I have a painting to work on.

I stood up,
Muttered to myself:
"I think I should start doing the frame."
Mother overheard this.

"It would be better than to just sit there - reading."
She commented.
We smiled.

I walked towards the sticks
Which I put out earlier that morning to dry.

The birds are chirping their lives away;
And so am I.

Crickets

The crickets are sounding the trumpets:

"Do Not Sleep Your Lives Away."

Whispers

First uttered word floats around

First utterance flowing

Like river gnawing the riverbanks.

Whispers can spread like a pungent perfume

Seemingly harmless whispers

Spoiling the day.

First word uttered

Flew like wind

Reaching ears far down south

Quarter to three down the bend.

Dull Colored Sky

Whispers pierce like bullets,
Trees bow down while I
Bent my body like a spoon.

I stretched out my hands
Towards the dull colored sky;
She flies around like a butterfly,
Beautiful as the dull colored sky.

Grievances

We fought and struggled,

To keep love;

To keep what we thought was ours.

We struggled and fought

Only to be silenced by loss and defeat.

We fought

Only to be silenced by defeat.

Green Board

"Writings on the wall
Green board like sheet
Weeping back at me."

Illogical

Why would I long for another heart?

I cannot think of any reason

I cannot think of anything else

Other than

"I am missing you".

Why would I long for another heart?

"I do not know."

Other than the illogical

"I am missing you".

Open Fire Nights

I wonder how some nights get to be so cold
If the heart is an open fire.

Gays

Gays
Let us talk about gays:

They are fun,
They make you laugh,
They can lift up the burdens of this world
And lift you up to greater heights.

Gays
They annoy me.
They need to be crucified.
For they have the ability to hide
From the harshness of the world.
I envy them for that.

To hell with them!

Envy
I guess that is the very thing
We should be talking about and not gays.

Gays are *gay* – alright.

At times we hate them;

For they make us hide.

They make us think:

I can never be like that.

I cannot be gay like that -

For always.

Story

You will have your turn
To tell your own story;
Yours will be told in a worn out
Piece of cloth.

Written words will spurt out
From the mouth of your pen.

You will have your turn.

Polished Green Eyes

From here to polished green eyes,

Ten years have passed.

Seemingly like yesterday.

Leaves descended like angels from the sky,

Devils stood like trees,

Branches reached out for mortality.

I ran like a coward;

The cattle stood up and ran like hell.

Hearts On Trees

If only hearts grow out on trees
I would have replaced mine in a blink of an eye;
Hence this painful throbbing inside would cease
To remind me of you.

If only hearts grow out on trees
I would not have to bother trying to forget you;
For all I need to do is replace this heart
That feeds on the memory of bygone days.

If only hearts grow out on trees
There will be no need
For tears and sad goodbyes;
No fear of having to spend
A life of without.

"If hearts grow out on trees,
I would have already replaced mine."

Hello

Were you lost when you said hello?
Or was it the laugh you heard

That made you come.

Pretty much the game of this world;
Lose or be lost to someone.

Pretty much the same to me.

Looking For God *(A Note to Paula)*

Do not go looking for God

In temples and churches;

You might end up recognizing God

As an idea that kill and cripple people.

Without

A life without you

is not a life at all;

But a misery

I need to sleep with every night.

The Face

Grain

If I were as tiny as a grain of sand

Would you notice me?

Would you pay attention

To the details of my life?

Or would you rather just pass me by;

As you would to a grain of sand

Lying on the ground.

I am a tiny heart that speaks;

For some reason I feel.

Behind Bars

Behind bars

I spoke of daffodils

And dreamt of you;

Behind closed doors

I screamed

For your presence.

I wept a hundred times

More than the days I have lived.

The thought of you

Is something no longer making sense.

Irony

There were like...

Thousands of things I hated about you.
Thousands of things I now look for in a woman.

This longing makes me sick to the stomach.
I need to wash you like a worn out muddy cloth.

Now, that is wishful thinking.

No matter how hard I try
There is only - you
In the middle of these heartbeats.

A beating heart no longer mine.

My Death

My death is when I stopped

Blinking in front of my wife.

Twisted limb flashes;

White faces melted like white chocolate.

This death keep things in check.

Holding back the dancer

Itching to dance

The dance of rebirth.

Somehow

Somehow

I feel

You are here

Only to bid farewell.

Stop

There are thousands of good reasons

Why write these things;

Countless good reasons why write

These things.

And 124 reasons

Why stop this non-sense.

Need Of Translation

AAN   HIN   MO

ANG   PANSAM ANTALANG

KALIGAYAHAN

K UNG   ANG

                              KATUMBAS

AY   HABAMBUHAY

NA

PAGKA MUHI

                    SA

          SARILI?

Cows

"WORK and they shall make cows and horses
out of you."

Onion Paper

A dishonest person walks in;

I laid my heart open

Like a blank sheet of onion paper.

Do Not

Do not look at me

Like you know me;

Do not talk to me

Like you know anything

About me.

Stop asking me

Like you really have something to say;

Do not even bother smiling at me

Nor even tap me on the shoulder.

It only makes me shudder.

In case you have forgotten

Enemies do not smile to one another.

Do not smile at me

It is not going to do us any good.

It is not going to bring

What has been lost.

Do not call me.

Nor tell my friends to say something about you.

Do not bother
Turning your head
Looking in this direction.

There is no point
In running after what is lost.
It is only going to take you back
Where we started.
A thought best left alone.

Enemies do not smile to one another
Remember?
In case you have forgotten.
Well, there you go -
I just reminded you of it.

Qatar

It is midnight light she said.
Her face covered with black silk.
It is strange
To be sitting right next to her

And yet feel the distance
Of our cultural differences

In galactic proportion.

I see only her eyes.

She is a strange woman with a beard;

In her black dress.

Quotes

Quote 1

Sometimes I think all I am is a heart.

Quote 2

Sometimes I think I don't have a heart.

Something

I feel like breaking something today;
Like breaking a glass or something.

My hands are shaking

Like it wants to break something
Like it wants something.

Something is brewing inside me.
I think it is the thought
Of being alone
Making me want to break something.

I need to distract the self
From realizing the loneliness
Solitude brings.

If only I have that something.

Sick

It sickens me
Thinking you can never be with me anymore.
You are taken.
Married to a stranger.

It sickens me thinking
I am sick.

Ill!
Sick!
Ill!

Sick to the stomach
This mustered courage of mine to tell you
How much I love you
Came too late;
Flickering and moaning like a dying buzz
In the garden of solitude.

Time

Let time pass over me,
Let the wind touching our faces,
Swift away our youth,
Our childish ways.

Time simply watches over
Not recognizing me.

I am the son
Of all the sons
Under the blue moon
Paper cut-out of man.

C. The Bells

It seems like there is no escaping you after all.

You seem to live inside my head.
Fluid.
Moving within my thoughts
Floating in circles.

I cannot catch up with you.

I need to get you out.
Out is where you should be.
Out of my head
So I could rest.

I have thought of killing myself
A hundred times already.
Just to escape you.

But here I am
Writing these words

Hoping it would make my head cease

From thinking about you.

But as you can see
It is not working.
Not at all.

Writing only made me think of you even more.

J

I hated the time we met
You reminded me so much of her.

Her alibis and excuses
Are tattooed on your lips.

And yet I want to be with you .
Spend a lifetime with you .
Hoping I can make it right this time.

Her weight does not bother me

Nor does it make me rethink

My sympathies and empathies

Over a ripped out heart.

Her weight is a presence

I keep sleeping with every night;

A sense of foreboding rippling in dreams

In the presence of her weightless volume.

Two Ways

There are two ways of dying in this life;

Falling in love is one.

The other is simply

Not doing anything about it.

Coffee Table Book

A constant reminder of your infidelity

Is my weakness to recognize it in the first few days of
exchanging words.

Your hand left a mark on my favorite coffee table
book.
I should not have let you borrow it in the first place.

A friend's note
Inserted in the middle of its pages
Says more than just that.
It says corruption of trust & decay of affection.

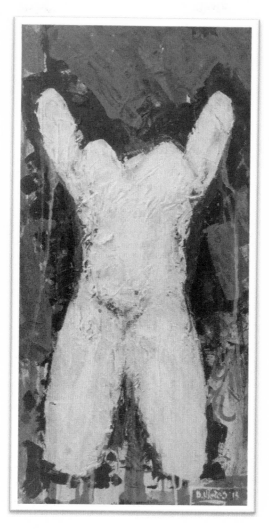

Bosom

Death Of A Star

The death of a star startled the whole town.
She walks like a ghost in the open air;
Whistling his name like a teapot.

Damn!
Was all they could say.
The death of her husband made her feel empty
And there was nothing anyone can do but watch

As tumbleweeds tumble around

Under the summer heat.

In The Middle

There is only I

In the middle of these heartbeats.

Hundreds and thousands of heartbeats;

Alone

In the middle of these.

Tiny Pieces

Tiny pieces of humanity

Hang around the corner of our eyes.

There is no sense in wearing

Your best dress

If you intend to milk a cow.

Flame

Inside

There is a flame burning inside me;

Not of excitement but of despair.

Not of joy but of sorrow.

A recognizable flame that is you.

A rusted blade stabbed straight into the heart

That is you as well.

That is how I remember you.

A flame and a rusted blade

Inside me I cannot seem to get rid of.

Curtains

Angels came rushing through the window;

Spitting glances to a child,

Giving her hope when there is none.

Leaves fell;

Curtains descended.

Darkness embraced the entire household.

Skinny

I over-consumed my heart:

The lamentation made it harder;

My thoughts about you made it harder.

The smell of summer

Smelled like your crack.

Your mouth spoke of plastic

While I remained skinny

Like I have always been.

Like I have always been.

Desert

She is the heart of the moving desert;
Plucked every single hope
From my tree.

My seeing eye;
My overseeing eye
Connecting me to the world.

In Dreams

People often times end up
With someone least expected;
For the men and women of our dreams
Exist only in dreams.

As youngsters we dream;
As adults worn out by time
We compromise.

Tired of waiting perhaps.

In The Cupboard

This longing I have over the times
Already lost
Is like a disease visiting me every night.
Questioning me.
Mocking me with devil's eyes.

I feel sorry for you and for us both.
I feel sorry for the times when we almost thought
We could have won.
In between those two opposing sides,
We only summoned failure.

In the cupboard there you hid
While I look for your face in the crowd.
In the secret closet of precious memories
There you wait for me to come and take you away
Once and for all.

This is failure mocking us
For eternity.

Porch

Past the meadows,

Trees and all,

Past the oceans,

Tides and all,

Past beauty and

Sickness and all;

Straight into the heart

Of an old man

Sitting in a porch

Watching toddlers crawl.

Hide and Seek

The kids were playing hide and seek
When she came in.

They were appalled by the look of her face.
Her face resembles that of the devil
And of all of the scary things they can think of.

"It is a disaster"
The kids say.

To look at that face with affection.
To look at the face of the devil with affection.

She is family now.
Even more scary.

Blue Sky

She is as wide as the blue sky above me;
Soft like clouds, fierce as claw.
Every time she speaks I tremble.

She is so beautiful - I tremble.

Cover

To long for what is lost

Is a frame of mind

I have become so accustomed with.

I feel old.

Enough to say

I have experienced

This grief a hundred times already.

A hundred times that always

Feels like the first time.

I really hate it

When all I can think about is you.

How I wish I can finally cover what is lost;

Like what I did with the old furniture

We used to own.

Dusty

Unclean

Dying to get lost.

Right Foot

"I extracted myself from the world;
The world tied itself to my right foot."

Pass

"Years passed like months,

Months passed like days;

Days passed like hours,

Hours passed like a dream."

Like Bonfires

After telling our stories we turned our backs
And walked away from what could have saved us
    from solitude.
We looked straight ahead
Kept walking
Without looking back
While bonfires burn
And later on died out that night.
Just like any other bonfire.

We told our stories to the campers
Whom we even forgot to ask the names.
But that won't be much of a problem, right?
Because most often than not, we just doesn't seem
    to care about details.
Faces will do; we hear ourselves say,
"We will remember their faces. "
It has always seemed to work that way

Elsewhere

"Yes, it is remarkable how sad moments
Could feel like a lifetime;
And how a push of a key could lead me to you;

In a fraction of a second,
I am suddenly elsewhere."

Murderer

My child died even before she was born; and for a while I was living with her murderer. Medusa was her murderer's name. A wonder of coldness and death.

Medusa cradled me to sleep for three years inside a jar that tasted like her crack. A taste of dirt and dust. A taste of dirt and death.

Now let me ask... Isn't it clear enough? I am a broken word of a father missing an unborn child; a murderer pretending to be a priest living amidst murderers. I have let a murderer love me thus making myself a murderer as well.

I miss my child. A child whose name is written in blood.

Property

"We do not own anything;
We never did and never will.
We cannot even keep our own lives
We are so proud calling ours."

Backdoor

At the back of my head
There is you
In your winter jacket;
In the cold
And in the absence
of my warmth.

I hope you die
Of cold and of lack of love one day.

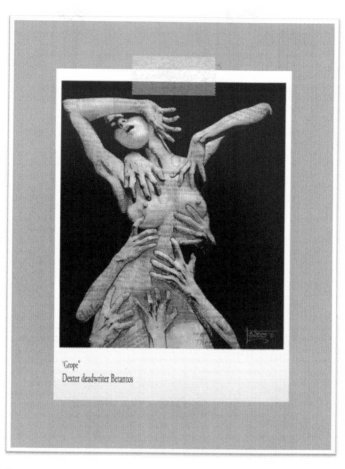

'Grope'
Dexter deadwriter Betantos

Grope

Amino Acid

Life offered me a chance today.
To excel;
To calculate;
To make haste;
To live.

I am burning with amino acid;
Grabbing me by the neck.

Her big lovely eyes screaming for me to make a move
While mine shuts for the better reason.

I should not let those lovely eyes
Gaze into mine.
For letting it do so will expose me;

"It is crazy to be true"
The sign says.

Better shut up now.

Thief

There is no escaping it now.

The kind of thief that takes your heart away

Is finally here.

She is here.

Now.

I just hope

This thief is staying for good this time.

Intentions

Not to forget
She said that is how she intends to keep it.

These words swirl inside my head
Clambering on between the crevices
Of my thoughts.
Intending to stay for a day
A week
More.

A lifetime.

Not to forget
That is how I intend to keep it.
To keep these broken words
And thoughts I have left of you
Inside me
Swirling.

Real Again

You were in my dream again last night.

Your face so real I can almost touch it.

Will it be like this for always?

This is torture.

A lifetime agony of waking up

In the middle of the night

Hoping I can make you real again.

It has been almost fifteen years now

And still you exist persistently in my dreams.

I must give up

Lose hope

I must dare myself to move.

I am dying a thousand deaths every time I go to sleep

For a love that exists only in dreams.

I love you so much it is burning me inside.

You are a dream that burns.

I know that now.

Kill A Phoenix

I must kill a bird.
A bird kindling this core made of cotton.

Kill this bird
I say.
Kill this Love.

Kill
The bird nesting inside.

Wishful thinking.
This bird is eternal
And will only be reborn out of flames
More fiery than ever.

This love cannot be killed.
It is like a phoenix.
I am sure it will rise out of the ashes again.

Eternally pushing me outside my comfort zone.
I am now a risk taker.

This time I will die trying.
I am certain of it.

Seeds

"Men are like seeds poured over

A floating rock in space;

Man must prove its worth and come into fruition

Or the display of magnificence

would be pointless."

One Chance

We only get one shot at this;
One shot at this life.
We are on probation;
Such is the arrangement with life.
One mistake and you will regret it;
That is the way of this life.

One chance is all we have
To make it right;
To do the things we want,
And to love the person we love.

One chance.

To love you,
To let you know how much I love you,
To be with you until I get old,
Was a one chance I wasted in this lifetime.

Improper

It has been two days since the last letter. Two days of waiting for an improper thing. I should call it obscene. Difficult. Disgrace. Failure. Loss and more. After all these years what I managed to achieve is become a failure at this thing called pursuit of happiness.

Her face is like a mirror staring back at me. Reminding me of the greatest loss in my life. Her lips speak silently of the unspoken words between us; her eyes, of the void in which I am in now.

Dream - that is what this life is for some. Including me. This is a dream. Living in wanting. Forever. For life. For eternity. For always.

Dot

There you go trying to make sense of it all
While I try to make sense of myself
Hoping to find reason in my wanting you back.

Waiting
When will this end?
When will this waking before every 3:00 a.m.
Of every single night cease?

I cannot even pull myself to get out of bed.

All I see is your face and that dot in the digital clock
That reminds me of you even more.

Confession

Confession of Compromise:

"A heart full of secret & bursting with tears is a sad heart wearing a smile."

Elegy Of Opposing Dreams

What is the weight of your first love

Compared to the next?

Or the ones that came after that?

Does it have the same weight as the first casual sex?

Or the second for that matter?

Or has it become weightless

Since man discovered casual sex?

The love of the 21st century is tainted

With fear & disgust.

A weightless elegy of opposing dreams.

Sons And Daughters

We are the sons and daughters of those who cannot
stare back.

The molested sons and daughters of the ones who are
no longer with us.

Our forefathers were the same;

They shunned away from the bleak truth.

Repeating lives a thousand fold

Like a story to strangers repeatedly told.

I can no longer find the rhythm in which I must reside
in order to be with you.

For I have grown into something staring back at

the eyes of bleak truth.

I no longer see the world the way I used to.

A floating spirit in the midst of a crowd

Of dried out souls walking around.

They say it is useless.

To notice it is uselessly useless.

A total waste of time,

For if to live life is to be happy then why look

At the face that would only cause you despair?

I am lonely as hell;

And I cannot find a reason not to.

Accuracy

Since I have not found you yet, I think it is accurate to say that I have been waiting all along in spite of my romantic affiliation with women other than you. When that time comes... when I finally find you, I will see those past rendezvous as mere rehearsals for the final play in the theater of *"Seek & love for life's sake."*

Never

You were there

Making life miserable for a kid

Who does not even know your name.

I saw you
Giving glances to that kid.

Let us wage war for love's sake
For life's sake.

But we cannot talk.
We should not.

Talking will make us lose our chance in life
Will make me want you more;
And that is not a chance
But a misery.

Damn you!
You made me feel almost wanted again.

Maybe it is time to kill this heart.
That should stop the longing for another heart
And I should never talk to you again.

Never.

Dandelions

She floats like a dandelion,

I - like a stone;

Heavy and a burden to the world.

She is a beauty that defines us all,

I – Slim like ore;

I break and bend for the world.

But it is okay.

- I have the TV -

While she has the beauty that defines us all.

Free Spirit

Free spirit is a wild bird;
Half of us do not have in our hearts.
I long to have it in mine,
For it to stay in my heart.

It is funny how a glance can make you doubt
Your decisions and make you question
The specifics of the journey you are taking.

Having trouble understanding what I mean?
That is exactly what I mean!

*"Being misunderstood and soaring high
  regardless of your opinion of me."*

Eighty

At the age of Eighty if we are lucky,
We shall start to understand life by then.

Purpose and Reason

Purpose & Reason...

Purpose & Reason.

Eternal searching in a world of dust.

Being a no-brainer could have been an option

If I had a say when God created me.

Once More

It is wrong
To think of you in the morning
Especially when I am lying next to her.

It is wrong
To wake up in the morning
Dreaming of your lovely face
And how you walk along with your friends
While I simply tag along with my gaze.

This is wrong
In so many ways.
To think
To long
To love
And to dream.

"Once More"

More than just letters.
They have become a lonely company

In the wee hours of the night.

Pikas

Cotton Candies

They say:

Cotton candies are found

In angels' bellies.

I say:

Angels are found

In cotton candy stalls.

Adagio

Inside me an adagio is playing.

While the rest of the world

Dances to the allegro of not knowing.

Stiffly Waiting

Where are you now?

Have we become so entangled with our current lives
That none of us dared looking back anymore?
It is a disaster when time provide in us
Only oblivious hearts.

I am stiffly waiting
In the crevice of a past love
Hiding

There is recognition in the spoken words
I tell you.
Upon the edge of losing you for good
I stand waiting for those same words
To come and blow me like a broken kite
Once again.

For the nth time.

Kim's Tree

Branches reach out for the sky
As the messenger take root.

Look, how I have grown now;
Look, how fully grown I am now.

As I take root,
My hand reaches out for the stars
Like a branch of a tree in a garden
Reaching out for the sky.

I was your tree
Still Am
I believe I am.

Destiny

Quite the opposite you said.
I cannot quite make out what you were saying
To your cousin.
About some old guy who lives behind the church
Was it?
Or was it about me being an old guy
Living behind my mother's couch?

Destiny.

It is such a deep word to play with.
We should inhibit ourselves from using it.
Not even in plain conversations.

It eradicates the sense of responsibility in a man.

Rip

The thought of it makes me warmer;

It makes me feel I can be whole again.

Mundane

Without formalities
Nor a need for one;
It is here
And it is now
I have come to live
The life I have been trying
To evade getting entangled with.

Mundane;

This curse of my own making
Screams at my face
Like a child screaming
At its own failure to climb
The hundred thousand steps
Of adolescence.

Mundane as it is
And recurring as it may seem

I am dying to get fixed.

Dying to get away from this life

I have come to live.

So mundane and lonely here

I feel like dying.

Unwashed Hands

Pungent smell of unwashed hands,
Fondle the breasts
Of the hungry women
Waiting to be touched.

Maybe, Move! Hope

Maybe not looking back

Would just do us good.

Maybe it is time to start moving our feet

To a different direction.

Maybe.

Move!

An ear - an inch away;

They will not hear this

They cannot hear this.

Move!

Is nothing but

A scream falling on a deaf heart

Refusing to move on.

Yes,

Swollen hearts cannot move on

Nor can it listen to words such as hope.

Sometimes forgetting

Can be such a foreign word

Tired hearts stop in trying

To understand it.

Smelt Fish

Out of the water

Tiny bodies

Only in winter.

Jewel

How many times

Will I go a-wandering?

How many more times

Will I go wondering about your beauty?

How many more 3:00 a.m. dreaming,

Will I find myself in?

Before I finally be awaken.

My Vacation

I held the refrigerator door open

Took out some string beans

Cut them to pieces

While mother talk non-sense.

About me I guess...

I guess we are making her

Proud of her children.

I took the string beans

Curtailed with the aid of my candle hands

While mother talk about her children

To some folk.

I guess we are making her proud.

Creases

"The creases on your pants are the very same creases of your own failures."

She said with her hands on her waist.

He just stood there in a daze.

He pretended

He did not hear anything

That is what he does - everyday.

While she screams her heart out like an officer

Shouting orders to a soldier lying in the pit

So afraid of getting killed.

"The creases on your pants are the very same creases of your failures."

Words repeated like a tired song on the radio.

A scene repeatedly playing in the household.

As tired eyes and hearts of the five children

Are forced to enjoy it as if it is enjoyable to watch.

Tonight

Tonight...

Sadness is my blanket.

Almost

Nine words were exchanged.
"I can be good."

She said
"I can be somebody. "

"I do not believe you"

Was all I could say to her.

Lies were written all over her face.

What she said in the nine word conversation

Made me feel miserable.

She made me feel almost wanted in life again.

Almost.

Now

Finally...

Here

is

Now.

Flight Ticket

I went to Dubai to see her
Then I met my wife and the mother of my children.

She was a face amongst the crowd of unfamiliar
faces.
Her smile I recognize since the skype days.
Her laugh made the fellows in the airport look with
intrigued eyes
Wondering about the smiles filling up the room.

9:07 p.m.
The time stopped.
I have my watch to prove that.

I came here to see a woman.
Instead I met the mother of my son.
The very same woman I came here for.

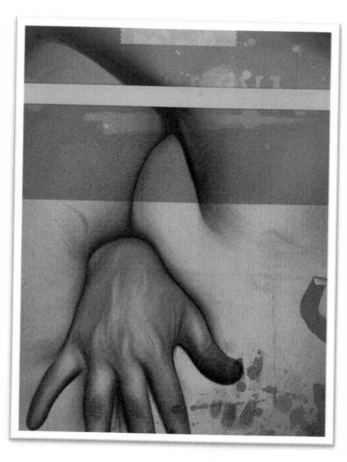

Curl

The paintings and illustrations of
Dexter *"deadwriter"* Betantos presented in this book
can be viewed in full color and detail in:
http://theartofdexterbetantos.webs.com
More literary works and support for this book in:
http://deadwriterdeadpoet.webs.com
Cover Design by Dexter "deadwriter" Betantos

ABOUT THE AUTHOR

Dexter deadwriter Betantos was born on March 11, 1979 in Maramag, Bukidnon, Philippines.

His love for art started at a very young age. Drawing inspirations from his comic books, he began drawing comic book characters. It was in the year 1998 and halfway through his college taking up Architecture when he decided to look for another way to express his artistic angst other than his paintings and illustrations. What he was looking for, he found it in writing. Realizing he only needed a pen and a piece of paper, be it the back of a receipt. "In writing one doesn't need a studio", "One simply write".

After college in 2001, he worked in a company exporting goods outside of the country, then later moved on to radio broadcasting and TV reporting in his hometown in 2003. In 2005 he worked as a Visual

Art Tutor in Manila. The following year, 2006, he returned to Mindanao and studied Secondary Education as his second course. He then started a career in secondary education, handling subjects such as English, Basic Computer, Social Studies and Advisory for the School Paper and Art Clubs until 2009 all the while studying for his Master's Degree in Educational Management. After three years of teaching he flew to Qatar and worked for a French Interior Designing company in 2010.

In 2012 he moved to Dubai. His writing became more engaged in the metaphysical, spiritual and philosophical. While working, he also sells his art online through a charity organization and takes joy in having enough to buy new art materials so he can continue painting.